Steam Memories: 1950's – 1960's

No. 42: East Coast Main Line

Compiled by **NEVILLE STEAD**

CW00525313

Copyright Book Law Publications 2011

ISBN 978-1-907094-63-7

INTRODUCTION

One of the foremost of Britain's railways always has been, and still is, the East Coast main line, connecting the capital cities of England and Scotland. Opened around 150 years ago by the linking of the Great Northern, North Eastern and North British railways, it has seen some of the best railway motive power in the country – from the Stirling 'Singles' of the 1870s, through the Ivatt 'Atlantic' era to the iconic Gresley 'Pacifics' of the 1920s and '30s. Further additions by Thompson and Peppercorn brought the Pacific fleet to a grand total of 202 locomotives by 1951.

This post-war period, which ended in the early 1960s with the arrival of the equally legendary 'Deltic' diesels, forms the background to a series of photographic books, with which I hope to re-kindle memories of those old enough, and perhaps educate younger readers about a golden age of steam power, before the inevitable march of progress produced today's high-speed electric trains.

The photographs are all from my negative collection, including a number around Holloway from the cameras of Arthur Carpenter and the late Roy Wilson – thank you gentlemen. Thanks are also due to David Percival for his knowledgeable assistance.

This is the first part of the journey north, from London (King's Cross) to Peterborough, so sit back and enjoy the ride.

Neville Stead, Whitley Bay, 2011

Cover Picture (See page 5)

Title Page Picture

It makes you wonder how a little engine can make so much smoke but there it is in black and white and various shades of grey. Ivatt J52 No.68888 battles up the grade through Holloway on 11th July 1953 with a Down freight. What was it like on the footplate in that tunnel?

Printed and bound by The Amadeus Press, Cleckheaton, West Yorkshire

First published in the United Kingdom by Book Law Publications, 382 Carlton Hill, Nottingham, NG4 1JA

In between its commuting duties, N2 No.69535 performed empty carriage working in and out of the terminus during its normal working day but is seen here at what appears to be platform 15 on the suburban – the local – west side of the station on Wednesday, 28th March 1956, the N2 had recently arrived back from a General overhaul at Doncaster where the usual lined black livery has given way to a drab austere black (although when it left the 'Plant' it was probably shiny black). Note the destination board placed upside down on the smokebox door but showing HIGH BARNET.

As seen from the York Road platform at the terminus, N2s Nos.69542 and 69497 have a mid-morning break at the stabling point established in the space between the portals of Gas Works tunnel. Just to the left of the photographer was another short stub of track used for stabling tank engines on e.c.s. duties at King's Cross – space at this place was certainly at a premium. The date is circa 1955 and both engines are looking reasonably clean. Except for the first three years after delivery to Hatfield, and nearly six months spent at Neasden during WW2, No.69542 spent most of its life working from 'Top Shed' whereas No.69497 was a King's Cross engine throughout.

Watched by just a few admiring souls, A4 No.60015 QUICKSILVER, with *THE ELIZABETHAN* on Monday 15th June 1959 – the first Down train of the season. This summer season non-stop express started life in 1949 as *THE CAPITALS LIMITED* but in 1953 its title was changed to honour the accession of Queen Elizabeth to the throne. Initially the journey time between London and Edinburgh was 405 minutes which changed to 390 during the second (1954) season. All the engines which hauled the train (excepting stand-ins for the not so frequent failure) were A4 class coupled to corridor tenders and allocated to either King's Cross or Haymarket sheds. As was usually the case, 34A have done a superb job with No.60015's exterior finish and the same could be said for its mechanical condition. One of the newly-introduced 'Baby Deltics' lurks in the shadow of the train shed to the left of the streamliner; now their mechanical condition was.....!!! But that's another story. *John Aylard.*

Another 'Top Shed' A4, No.60033 SEAGULL, flaunts its clean and elegant lines at King's Cross whilst awaiting departure with *THE SCARBOROUGH FLYER.* It is August 1959 and the express has some special motive power for a change on this day although King's Cross shed supplied the motive power for the Down train and usually provided something clean. York was responsible for the engine of the Up train and all sorts from V2, A1, and A2 were used with the occasional visiting A3 or A4 thrown into the mix. No matter what class of engine hauled this train, it still took a long time to get from London to Scarborough because of both the timings (nearly five hours either way) and the engine change at York where B1s or B16s and sometimes D49s, were used for the last leg to the coast. In latter BR days, before its total demise in September 1962, the train ran only on Fridays and Saturdays to Scarborough with Saturday and Sunday return workings.

The unmistakable lines of the Gresley A3 are perhaps more associated with King's Cross than any other steam locomotive. This is Doncaster based No.60064 TAGALIE arriving at the terminus in 1953 with an express from Yorkshire.

Peppercorn A1 No. 60114 W.P.ALLEN arrives at 'The Cross' on Wednesday 4th May 1949 with the 9.50 a.m. express from Leeds. The presence of a dynamometer car in the train was to test the drawbar horsepower of the A1 against that given out by A2 No.60539 which worked this same train on the following day. The apparent load was 490 tons and both engines ran superbly with the A1 recording 2,108 h.p. whilst the smaller-wheeled A2 indicated slightly more. The following week No.60114 took part in four daily trials between London and Grantham and return where the trailing load was notched up to more than 600 tons each way. The A1 sailed through all those eight tests with flying colours – what did you expect. Note the precise 'bulling up' of the engine, with both 'Top Shed' and Copley Hill depots involved in the turn-out of the Pacific.

Another safe arrival at King's Cross terminus. On a busy afternoon in 1962 A1 No.60158 ABERDONIAN stands alongside platform 2 with the *YORKSHIRE PULLMAN. John Aylard.*

Mentioned earlier, this is the other stub siding used for stabling engines on the east side of the station. No.69584 appears to be engaged in shunting parcels stock (note the Continental wagon) at platform 1, although the destination board on the smokebox door shows evidence of other employment with a 'local' to Hertford North on the loop line. This view of the terminus, from the York Road station platform on some unknown date in the 1950s, shows the two arched train sheds, the signal box which oversaw everything, and in the distance the roof of neighbouring St Pancras. The line nearest the platform served not just the York Road and King's Cross No.1 platforms but continued south-eastwards (off picture to the left) into a tunnel to connect with the eastbound Metropolitan and Circle Lines. That particular connection has long since been taken out of use, the York Road platform closing in November 1976.

A further aspect of the terminus in the late Fifties with 34A's own V2, No.60800 GREEN ARROW, departing platform 5 with an afternoon express for Peterborough. Note that the first two vehicles are Gresley articulated stock.

A3 No.60063 ISINGLASS receives some attention at King's Cross 'Top Shed' on 6th May 1955. This particular A3 was a recent addition to the 34A stud after a two year stint working the former Great Central route from Neasden shed. A bit of a wanderer, the engine moved back to Neasden in March 1956 but then returned to King's Cross after a couple of months before moving north to settle down at Grantham. Note the immaculate QUICKSILVER alongside.

The coaling plant at King's Cross on 9th May 1954 with New England A2/3 No.60513 DANTE being topped-up. The visiting Pacific looks fairly clean for a 35A engine whereas the local fleet (judging from the N2s on the right) were amongst the dirtiest on the ECML. However, things were to change at King's Cross when a new Shed Master took over the reins and cleaning standards were changed for the better with all of the fleet – not just the Pacifics – getting regular cleaning.

A4 No.60021 WILD SWAN appears ready for another northbound working in this 22nd February 1962 view at King's Cross shed. The end was in sight for 34A with just sixteen months to go before total closure. Most of the remaining serviceable locomotives were then sent to New England or Grantham. The end for this A4 came shortly afterwards in October 1963.

We have moved north to Holloway now, the main line getting a good airing after being in two lots of tunnels and a deep cutting. Here the incoming goods trains for King's Cross goods depot were taken by a flyover from the east side of the passenger lines to the west thereby allowing the passenger traffic to work in and out of the terminus without disruption from slow freights crossing their paths. As it was, the arriving (Up) passenger services were often held up anyway between Hornsey and the terminus so if this flyover had not been provided the delays would have been even worse than they were. Coming up the grade on 9th May 1954 is A4 No.60014 SILVER LINK with the 10.21 a.m. to Cambridge. Note that not all of 34A's charges were filthy at this time.

Seen emerging from Copenhagen tunnel on the Down main, A4 No.60025 FALCON has charge of the 10.35 a.m. to Leeds, Bradford and Harrogate on 11th July 1953. The chime whistle has just sounded and someone in the cab (it may well have been a locomotive inspector, looking at the collar and tie) is leaning out to look ahead. This aspect of the Holloway layout shows the point where the Up goods line leaves the flyover and dives into the third bore of the Copenhagen tunnels.

On Sunday 9th May 1954, Doncaster based A3 No.60109 HERMIT had charge of the 10.00 a.m. from King's Cross to Edinburgh. Climbing the Down main, the Pacific was not looking to be in top condition, either externally or mechanically.

On 11th July 1953, New England V2 No.60966 climbs the gradient of the Down main with the Saturday service of *THE NORSEMAN*. This boat train had been part of the ECML fabric since the 1920s and like all express passenger services in the United Kingdom suffered during the 1939-45 war but because of its maritime connections its viability took a little longer to be accepted so its post-war place in the timetables was slow to materialise. By 1950, with regular twice-weekly sailings from the Tyne to Norway taking place, the train's recovery got to the point where BR ran a twice weekly – Tuesday and Saturday – return service between King's Cross and Tyne Commission Quay via Newcastle (Central). Intended for embarking passengers only, and departing King's Cross at 9.10 a.m., the train, complete with restaurant car, ran non-stop to York to pick-up passengers for a 2.53 p.m. arrival at the quayside on the Tyne.

Seen from the Up goods flyover, B17 No.61652 DARLINGTON rounds the curve at Holloway with the Up 9.18 a.m. *CAMBRIDGE BUFFET EXPRESS* on Saturday 11th July 1953. Once known as the *GARDEN CITIES AND CAMBRIDGE BUFFET EXPRESS* and carrying appropriate roofboards on the rolling stock, the locomotives never actually carried a headboard – it would have been somewhat large. When the service was inaugurated in 1932, five trains each way ran between Cambridge and King's Cross each day, stopping at Welwyn Garden City, Hitchin and Letchworth. Amongst Cambridge undergraduates they were popular and became known as the Beer Trains. WW2 put a stop to the service but resumption by the LNER, post-war, saw the service eventually reach four each way per day. However, the fastest pre-war timings of one hour and twelve minutes were never reached, never mind bettered, the best being 80 minutes. The train's name was also shortened to the last three words only but the three intermediate stops were kept and in some cases more were introduced.

An interesting view of the three tunnel mouths at Holloway as seen from the Up goods flyover. On the Down main Thompson B1 No.61095 emerges into the sunshine on that July Saturday in 1953 with the 11.00 a.m. express to Peterborough.

With the gradient of Holloway bank letting gravity do the pushing, J50 No.68985 keeps a tight hold of an Up freight on Wednesday 8th July 1953. With its poles just visible, note the trolleybus proceeding north along Caledonian Road bridge.

A1 No.60114 W.P.ALLEN hurries out of Copenhagen tunnel, passes beneath the Up goods flyover and makes for the open air at Holloway as it proceeds north along the Down main with the 5.35 p.m. King's Cross- Newcastle (Central) on Tuesday 11th May 1954. It is a weekday evening and the northbound main line procession would have started some time ago but the local commuter services are just getting into their stride.

N2 No.69582 traversing the Down slow line at Holloway with the 9.30 a.m. to Hertford North on 11th July 1953, employing two Quad-Articulated sets outside the rush hour, so presumably with a more modest complement of passengers. Note the allotments straddling the gentle slope of the embankment – a location some of us might have found to be idyllic.

23

Still at Holloway but going back to Tuesday 11th May 1954, J50 No.68987 is taking empty carriage stock to 'The Cross' for the evening rush. Next to the J50 is a Gresley steel-panelled non-gangway twin brake composite.

On to Finsbury Park now where we are just in time to watch A3 No.60065 KNIGHT OF THISTLE make the station shudder as it runs through platform 4 with an express for King's Cross on 8th July 1953. As stations go, Finsbury Park was quite large inasmuch that it had ten platform faces on five island platforms. In the background can be seen the flyover carrying the Alexandra Palace branch whilst just beyond that are the arches of Endymion Road bridge. Our scruffy Pacific was a Grantham engine at this time in its life but it ended its days at New England during the final week of June 1964.

25

Proceeding north through Harringay on 5th October 1957, we come across this viaduct shortly after passing through the station. J52 No.68846 (apparently) has charge of a freight bound for the North London line from Ferme Park Down yard on the left of the picture. Somewhere in the distance through the bridge spans can be seen Hornsey engine shed whilst to the right are the Up sidings where so much of London's coal arrived from Derbyshire, Nottinghamshire and Yorkshire. The Down yard sorted goods from the Southern Region and many a locomotive with a five digit number starting with 3 has passed through here.

A quick visit to Hornsey engine shed on 3rd October 1954 reveals the usual batch of N1 tanks with No.69458 amongst the throng. Hornsey's 0-6-2Ts not only handled local passenger services and empty stock workings but also had a hand in the inter-regional freight movements with the Southern Region. Hornsey N1s could be found at Hither Green for instance on a daily basis. No.69458 was by this date getting on a bit and had just one year of operational life left before its final visit to Doncaster. Throughout its near forty-five year life, the N1 had worked mostly from Hornsey, the exceptions being three years at Hatfield during WW2 and two years in post-war Bradford. 27

Hornsey station had nowhere near the number of platforms found at Finsbury Park but it offered the same main line traffic but fewer commuter trains. However, many of the freights working in from the north only got as far as Hornsey because they terminated at Ferme Park yards where they would be broken up and sent to various parts of London and the south-east. Serviced, turned and made ready to work back to whence they came, their locomotives had no need to venture further south than this place. The draw for the local spotters though remained the Pacifics and one young lad notes the name of Peppercorn A1 No.60139 SEA EAGLE as its hurries through Hornsey with a heavy Up express in late August 1958 – happy days!

Looking north from the footbridge seen in the background of the previous illustration, Hornsey carriage sidings are seen in the distance with at least two engines at the head of empty stock. Coming towards the camera is J50 No.68979 with a lengthy rake of stock for King's Cross. The procession of e.c.s. workings must have seemed endless. No sooner had one lot arrived from the terminus when another lot was required - an endless and fascinating conveyor belt which only slowed down during the small hours. The main line lies just beyond the 0-6-0T and its train. Already the main line, empty carriage and goods lines have been segregated with the goods lines for Ferme Park yards taking the tracks to the right thereby by-passing the station. Two underbridges, or at least their parapets, are in view; the nearest spans the New River, a man-made watercourse designed to supply water to north and east London from a source near Hertford! The tower of the Metropolitan Water Board's (Hornsey Waterworks) pumping station is just visible behind the exhaust of the J50. The next bridge spans a main road, which was even busier than the railway. Beyond that, and to the right of the carriage sidings is the local Gas Works, another customer for the railway – at least it was then – taking a large quantity of coal on a regular basis. The date has been lost but it is certainly summertime and probably circa 1957.

Still looking north from the Hornsey footbridge but a little later the same day. We now see N2 No.69577 working an Up local comprising two quad-art sets. The air is slightly clearer now, the N2, with a lighter load, not required to work as hard as the J50. In the distance an Up freight has arrived and is blowing off on the main line whilst waiting for the signal to proceed southwards. Our vantage point is the second such bridge to span this section of the Hornsey complex. The first bridge, dating from 1900, was destroyed completely during a German air raid in WW2 and was not replaced until the start of the BR period. There is no doubt about it though, we have been lucky that certain photographers took the trouble to capture on film scenes such as these whereby a realisation, and appreciation, of the railway system, which probably reached its zenith shortly after Nationalisation, can be gained. Nowadays the modern railway is less crowded, less expansive, tidier, quieter, and cleaner. For all that it is also less interesting.

On to Wood Green now and we catch J6 No.64266 heading back to Hornsey engine shed on Saturday 27th March 1954. The 0-6-0 is waiting at the signals at the south end of Wood Green station. The footbridge framing the engine is another with a bit of history. It was erected by the Great Eastern Railway in order to give intending passengers from nearby Palace Gates station a fairly direct route to the racecourse situated immediately south of the GN station, at Alexandra Palace.

To liven up the Wood Green station precincts, a Down Leeds express rattles through on 1st July 1949 with Copley Hill A3 No.60056 CENTENARY in charge. With at least fourteen vehicles on, the Pacific has got its work cut out. Already the gas holders at Hornsey are receding and we are slowly leaving 'The Smoke' behind although there is still much of this great metropolis to navigate before we reach open country.

Summer 1955, Wood Green station, early evening 12th July 1955. Out of nowhere comes A4 No.60013 DOMINION OF NEW ZEALAND with the Down *YORKSHIRE PULLMAN*. Some of the train's passengers are perhaps already dining, others would certainly be having an aperitif beforehand. By the time they all get home in three hours or so, it will be just getting dark but their working day would have been finished off with a comfortable northbound journey, enjoying a certain experience that is no longer available on Britain's railways.

From Friday 12th to Sunday 14th September 1958, British Railways held an exhibition at Noel Park goods yard in Wood Green as part of the Charter celebrations of the Borough of Wood Green. Amongst the engines 'laid on' by BR were these two tanks: C12 No.67352 and J52 No.68846 which, as can be seen, were certainly turned-out to exhibition standard. Afterwards the J52 carried on as normal but the Atlantic tank made its way, via a stint at Grantham, to Doncaster where it was broken up!

It is getting on into late evening now in July 1949 but the trains are still thick and fast around Wood Green. Just north of the station – well some distance beyond – A3 No.60108 GAY CRUSADER is seen running north and about to enter Wood Green tunnel with an express. Note the N2 crossing the so-called New Line flyover with a train for the Hertford loop stations. The loop line was regularly used as a diversionary route on Sundays, and a time of accidents on the main line. Meanwhile, the Down slow has another N2 running under clear signals trying to match the Pacific! So, we leave another station and a couple of commuter trains behind us as we continue along the ECML.

Having sped through New Southgate we reach the deep cutting embracing Oakleigh Park station where we meet an Up express headed by Thompson A2/3 No.60523 SUN CASTLE on the rather crisp and sunny early afternoon of Saturday 28th February 1953. By now the station layouts have become much less elaborate with only two island platforms required to serve all the running lines. Oakleigh Park station dates from 1873 and is still operational.

Just south of the station on the same afternoon, B17 No.61623 LAMBTON CASTLE gallops through the cutting with a well loaded Down *CAMBRIDGE BUFFET EXPRESS.*

This rather delicate looking footbridge which was in sight of the Oakleigh Park platforms, and situated at about the 8-mile marker south of the station, perhaps mid-way to Barnet tunnel, was certainly a focal point for the local trainspotters judging by the numbers gathered. A rather grubby Thompson L1, No.67800, is making its way towards King's Cross on the Up main, something that local trains were allowed to do this far out of town during quiet periods. The date is 20th September 1953 – a Sunday with not a lot to excite these youngsters except perhaps the thrill of seeing a distant signal indicate that something was coming. However, this was the day when 'Atlantics' 990 and 251 worked a special from King's Cross to Doncaster!

We are now at New Barnet and just in time to observe A4 No.60003 ANDREW K.McCOSH proceed through the station with the 3.15 pm King's Cross- Niddrie express goods (also known since LNER days as the Scotch Goods although scheduled then for a 3.40 p.m. departure from King's Cross). We have no date for this image but it is probably circa 1960 as the Pacific has ATC/AWS fitted but has not yet acquired the speed indicating gear nor those electrification warning flashes.

39

We are at the end of the four-track section by Greenwood box where the 'squeeze' for Hadley Wood tunnels began. Putting up a good turn of speed and with nothing to impede its progress at this point, a Down Cambridge express proceeds north behind B17 No.61624 LUMLEY CASTLE on Thursday 4th October 1951. At this time the whole class were resident at six former Great Eastern sheds; Cambridge having a sizeable allocation numbering seventeen engines, second only to Stratford's eighteen. This particular engine became only the second B17 to be condemned, an event which took place on Monday, 16th March 1953 at Doncaster 'Plant' works. Note the platelayers trolley stabled on the sleepers at the end of the trap.

Seven months after the previous view was recorded, and from a ground level perspective, a Cambridge stopping train headed by Thompson B1 No.61139 hurries north at Greenwood on Friday 16th May 1952. Waiting at the signal on the Down Slow N2 No.69490 has charge of an empty stock train. It was this continuous delay to trains, especially commuter trains which spurred the boring of a second set of tunnels between here and Potters Bar, albeit some years after this event.

Still at Greenwood on that Friday evening but no sign now of any delays to local traffic as Peppercorn A1 No.60144 KING'S COURIER heads the Down *WEST RIDING*, sans headboard. Note that six of the original streamlined *WEST RIDING LIMITED* carriages were included in this British Railways service, all at the front end of this formation.

Not all of the Cambridge semi-fasts were six-coupled hauled. This Cambridge-King's Cross working, passing through Hadley Wood on 19th July 1952, has Cambridge allocated D16/3 No.62618 in charge. Note the ballast ready for refreshing the Up line, long before any widening works were begun.

Hadley Wood, Saturday 19th July 1952, some seven years before the quadrupling of the main line. Peppercorn A1 No.60122 CURLEW strides out for the seaside with *THE SCARBOROUGH FLYER*. The wayside station, still in its original GN as-built condition of 1885, sits comfortably in the Green Belt north of the Capital. Once the Down train has passed a relative calm would descend over this place until the next train rushed through. There are, as yet, no BR corporate image signposts, lamps or indeed anything to give a clue as to the era. On the right, hidden by the fencing, was a small coal yard but that was later swallowed up during the widening works, the two lines stabling wagons for the local coal merchants effectively becoming the new Down fast and slow lines albeit with new formation. Much of the original station booking hall and ticket office was retained for the new four-track station although extensively modernised internally.

At a date unknown but thought to be in the late summer of 1959, V2 No.60903 bursts out of Hadley Wood South tunnel with a Down relief. The still pristine concrete and brickwork around the tunnel mouth and the retaining walls would suggest that the completion of the widening had only just taken place in the previous few months or even weeks. Therefore, August 1959 would be near to the actual date and, to further the evidence, No.60903 had just completed a 'General' at Doncaster in mid-March when AWS was fitted. The condition of the engine is still quite commendable but it was a 34A charge anyway, so external condition was not always a clue regarding ex-works dates. 45

Heading a Down local passenger working, N2 No.69546 leaves the first of the tunnels behind as it slows for the stop at Hadley Wood in July 1959. When the construction phase of the widening work was completed in March 1959 there remained the small problem of changing over the railway from two to four track working. This was achieved over the five weekends between 4th and 5th April and 2nd, 3rd and 4th May. During that period the new Down slow was brought into use on 4th April as the temporary Down fast and by 27th April the tracks through the original tunnels were converted to Up slow and Up fast whilst the new Down fast was brought into use on 4th May, the last bit of the jigsaw. The new tunnels are circular and lined throughout with concrete segments – cast in a specially built facility nearby – being used instead of the more traditional brick lining; the latter ruled out at the early stages of planning simply because of the expense and short supply. Ironically, the tunnels were driven through clay and what are bricks made of! The spoil from all three bores was taken in hoppers by a 2ft-gauge railway to a 25-acre site at Ganwick Farm, between Hadley Wood North and Potters Bar tunnels. Even then, in the mid-Fifties, consideration was given to the contours of the tip and its finished condition and when dumping was completed, top soil was laid followed by grass seed; and that was over fifty years ago!

Another weekend for holiday trains – Saturday 2nd August 1952 – and A3 No.60039 SANDWICH bursts out of Hadley Wood North tunnel at Ganwick with *THE SCARBOROUGH FLYER*. The Pacific would work the train to York where a usually less than pristine 50A six-coupled engine would take the train on to the coast. Of the three tunnels involved with the Potters Bar widening, this particular bore was the shortest at 232 yards, Hadley Wood South being 384 yards, whilst Potters Bar tunnel was a respectable 1,214 yards long.

A little further to the north of the last image, we see A3 No.60080 DICK TURPIN in the stretch of open country between the Hadley Wood North and Potters Bar tunnels at Ganwick. The date is 14th April 1949 and the resplendent Heaton based Pacific – just out of Doncaster from a General overhaul and in LNER green too – has charge of the Down *TEES-TYNE PULLMAN*. The new railway to be laid through here would set down two lines in the space between the train and the photographer, these becoming the Down fast and slow lines. Altogether more than two and a half miles of new railway was created to eliminate this notorious bottleneck.

Exiting Potters Bar tunnel on Friday 29th July 1949, King's Cross A4 No.60017 SILVER FOX, in LNER Garter blue livery but with 'British Railways' on the tender, is in charge of the Down *YORKSHIRE PULLMAN.* **British Railways were trying their best to accelerate these business trains in order to win back traffic.**

Long before the Potters Bar widening was started to alleviate the bottleneck between Greenwood and Potters Bar, another 'Top Shed' A4 No.60003 ANDREW K. McCOSH, also still in LNER Garter blue, brings the Down *TEES-TYNE PULLMAN* up the grade towards Potters Bar station on Friday 29th July 1949. This train was introduced by British Railways in September 1948 in order to attract the business clientele which had used the pre-war *SILVER JUBILEE*. Timings were nowhere near the streamliners' four-hour dash but they had been cut to five hours during the previous May and in the following September to just four hours and fifty-five minutes, London to Newcastle, with a stop at Darlington! Departure time from King's Cross was 4.45 p.m. – the slot had been given up by the *YORKSHIRE PULLMAN* which was put to a 5.30 p.m. departure. The speed was not quite there but the touch of luxury certainly was. The A4 haulage was not an accident either so the eight vehicles were easy enough for the trusty Pacific and only the track needed sorting out to bring further cuts in time.

Another Friday evening express for the north approaches Potters Bar in glorious sunshine in July 1949. This is the Down Hull with A3 No.60055 WOOLWINDER in charge. Making a bit more smoke than either of the A4s we have just seen, the A3 had a slightly heavier load. On arrival at Doncaster, the Pacific will be replaced by a Hull Botanic B1 or perhaps a D49 but this Friday loading would more likely attract the Thompson engine.

Potters Bar and South Mimms station, pre-widening. We are just over twelve miles out from King's Cross now as we meet a somewhat dirty and as yet unnamed Peppercorn A1, No.60118, heading towards London with the Up *YORKSHIRE PULLMAN* on Thursday 4th August 1949. Only nine months old at the time of the photograph, No.60118 was allocated to Copley Hill. Its livery was apple green - you will have to take my word for it - but in May 1950 it was afforded BR blue prior to being named ARCHIBALD STURROCK. By January 1952 BR returned the engine to green livery – Brunswick green – a colour in which it ran until withdrawal in October 1965. What of the station? As mentioned earlier, this traffic bottleneck was to be opened out during the next five years and the quaint old GNR station, dating from August 1850, was swept away and replaced by a modern concrete and glass station with two island platforms.

On to Welwyn Garden City where we meet a heavy Up express rolling through the station, circa 1960, with a filthy Grantham based A3, No.60102 SIR FREDERICK BANBURY, in charge. Despite the external appearance, the Pacific seems to be mechanically sound.

Returning from Blackbridge tip, N7 No.69649, a newcomer to Hatfield shed, runs past the Down island platform at Welwyn Garden City with a rake of empty open wagons which had formed a rubbish train trip on Thursday 22nd July 1954. The station here was the newest on the line and, opening in 1926, was built to serve the newly created (1920) Garden City which was founded by town planner Ebenezer Howard, who was later knighted. The second such garden city in England, WGC is some twenty miles from London, and the population now numbers more than 43,000 souls. The tip mentioned in the opening sentence was situated on the single line branch to Luton and Dunstable, which diverged from the main line just beyond the plate girder bridge carrying a public road and which was also the site of the first Welwyn Garden City station opened for public use in August 1920 but which had origins back to 1858. Despite appearances, the N7 and its infamous 'smelly' train is not running 'wrong line' but on the branch single line which extended to Hatfield, next to the Down slow line.

The King's Cross-Niddrie goods gets the Down main through Welwyn G.C. on the afternoon of 22nd July 1954. New England V2 No.60874 takes the train on its first stint (to Doncaster) where a Doncaster engine would take over for the run to York. About a half mile south of the station can be seen the arches of what is known locally as 'Twentieth Mile' bridge.

22nd July 1954 again and still at Welwyn Garden City where a Thompson B1, No.61393 of King's Cross shed, is ready for the off with a Down Cambridge working.

Another Hatfield N7, No.69637 finishes off a spot of shunting at Welwyn on that Thursday in July 1954. The Up fast is signalled for an express and the very same can just be made out coming beneath the arched bridge to the north.

Fresh from shops and going flat-out, Cambridge based B17 No.61640 SOMERLEYTON HALL is captured on film crossing Digswell (Welwyn) viaduct on Saturday 17th April 1954 with a Down *CAMBRIDGE BUFFET EXPRESS*. This particular viaduct is one of the more well known structures found on the ECML although to take full advantage of its architectural appeal you have to stand in the valley of the River Maran (also known as Mimram) which is traversed by the viaduct. At this time the 4-6-0 was running with a Diagram 100 boiler which effectively put it in class Part 2 but in May of the following year it emerged from Doncaster works with a 100A boiler which then put it in class Part 6. During November 1958, in what turned out to be its final visit to the 'Plant', No.61640 was condemned and afterwards cut up. The viaduct, situated between Welwyn Garden City and Welwyn North stations, and only slightly disfigured by catenary, is still going strong and will hopefully continue to do so for another one hundred and fifty-odd years.

We are just at the twenty-two mile post now standing on the Up platform at Welwyn North station with WD Austerity 2-8-0 No.90158 making good progress with a very heavy Down freight on 17th April 1954. One of New England's large allocation of 'Austerities', No.90158 spent much of its BR life working on the ECML. Welwyn North was another of the 1850-built GNR stations which remained unaltered for more than a century; the North suffix was added in 1926.

With Peppercorn A1 No.60157 GREAT EASTERN at its head, an Up express leaves Welwyn South tunnel behind and is bearing down on Welwyn North station at more than a mile a minute. It is 19th July 1954 and this view from the footbridge at the south end of the station gives a reasonable aspect of the GNR structures and the cutting containing the station and its small goods facility. Note that the platform edges have been recently renewed. Is that timber shelter on the Down platform original GN?

We are now some thirty-two miles from London at Hitchin – junction for the Cambridge line – on 16th April 1952. At first glance a stranger to this section of the ECML might think they are somewhere on the Midland route but this is pure Great Northern country. 3F 0-6-0 No.43766 is slowly making its way through Hitchin station on the Up slow with a goods train from Bedford. The Midland Railway had arrived in Hitchin in 1857 via a direct line from Bedford. Up to the opening of St Pancras in 1868 all the Midland passenger traffic from the provinces to London came through that route from Bedford to Hitchin and along the ECML to King's Cross. The MR even built an engine shed at Hitchin – two in fact – but its presence after 1868 was more rudimentary with an engine or two showing up each day on a goods turn such as this and on passenger workings. The engine shed itself was closed by the LMS but the yard facilities, including the turntable, were in use until 1960. Nowadays there is no sign of the MR connection to Hitchin but for more than a century, Midland and LMS locomotives worked the line from Bedford.

There is no record as to what this train is standing in Hitchin's Up platform on Thursday 15th July 1954 but it may be a stopping train from Cambridge. The star of the piece is the A4, a fairly respectable looking No.60015 QUICKSILVER from 34A. On the Down platform a porter sits on the edge of a barrow stacked with mail bags. The picture has the feel of evening so that lot may have been the sorted last post. Behind this platform, just over the wall, was the two-road engine shed which had served Hitchin since the day the Great Northern Railway opened its main line between London and Peterborough – 7th August 1850. It was looking a bit dilapidated by July 1954 but it still had a few more years of hosting not only its own allocation but also the occasional main failures which were usually sorted out by the lads at 34D.

When was the last time you saw four station staff members within twenty yards of each other but all going about their own separate tasks? This is Hitchin Down platform on Wednesday afternoon, 8th July 1953 with a Down outer-suburban train. The train engine is Thompson L1 No.67743, one of Hitchin's own batch of nine which had been at the place since late 1948. In conjunction with the King's Cross batch they ran most of the outer-suburban and semi-fast passenger traffic between Hitchin and the Capital for much of the 1949-58 period.

Sixty-nine miles out from London now. This is Holme station on Saturday 4th April 1959 just two days before it was closed. We are looking north towards the point where the branch to Ramsey (some five miles to the east) veers away to the right of the main line. Opened in August 1850, this Huntingdonshire station was approximately half a mile east of the village (population 1948: 614; twice the number recorded when the railway first arrived) of the same name, connected by the B660 – appropriately named Station Road. The B660 crossed the ECML by level crossing, the normal means of getting passengers and luggage between platforms. That this station remained open to 1959 seems incredible because the passenger service on the Ramsey branch was discontinued in October 1947. Besides the station goods yard, tucked away on the Down side behind the goods shed, a bank of sidings can be seen in the distance situated between the main line and the branch. The shiny rails on the east side of the island platform show plenty of run-round activity had been taking place up to this actual day. Goods activity on the branch was to continue for many years yet. Rather than milk, the churns on the Up platform probably contained water for the various isolated signal boxes south of this place and would be collected by either a local pick-up goods or light engine, the latter sent out from New England especially to do the job.

Whilst we are at Holme we will take a five mile detour from the ECML to see what was left of the terminus of the branch line to Ramsey. It is still Saturday 4th April 1959 and we are at the site of the former Great Northern station which was opened in July 1863 by the Holme & Ramsey Railway Co. At first the terminus was of a temporary nature but within twelve months a permanent installation was operating. The line was to be worked by the Great Northern and an engine shed was erected by the Ramsey Co. for the branch engine, which was out-stationed from Peterborough and changed weekly by way of a twice weekly Ramsey-Peterborough passenger service. The engine shed went out of use in 1885 by which time the Great Eastern Railway, which had purchased the branch in 1870, had leased the line to the GN. The branch was then worked on the one engine in steam principle up to closure with a daily engine from Peterborough working the branch as necessary. As mentioned earlier, passenger traffic to this place ceased in October 1947 but a daily goods service continued as evidenced here by a New England J6 shunting the terminus. Although the goods shed was minuscule compared to most, the yard contained a 5-ton crane which can be seen on the dock beyond the shed. The GER had its own terminus at Ramsey East (renamed High Street and approximately half a mile from the GN station) which included passenger and goods facilities and an engine shed too. That particular branch, which opened in 1889, ran from Somersham and it was the original intention of the GER to link the two termini, however, the LNER decided that the GE line was the less profitable of the two and closed that branch in 1930.

The view to the north-west from the Ramsey terminus on that 4th April 1959 with the J6 now departed to Holme and then New England. There was one intermediate station on the branch at St Mary's, situated about a third of the distance from Ramsey to Holme. At its height, just before Grouping, the branch managed seven return passenger trains daily, three in the morning and four after noon. After working the last train from Holme to Ramsey, the branch engine picked up the goods wagons at the terminus whilst leaving the passenger stock overnight. Next morning the first train on the branch would be the goods from Peterborough which, after running round at Holme, would arrive in Ramsey in time to work the first passenger service of the day to Holme, departing at some time before 7.00 a.m. Shunting the goods yard would take place between passenger turns. Besides what we can see in this view, the goods facilities extended onto the southern boundary of the site, a large three storey stone-built warehouse, complete with hoists and used for agricultural storage. Note the post-war prefab building which apparently had a short career serving as passenger station offices, later becoming the goods office. It lasted until closure of the site but was demolished soon after. The large stone warehouse is still apparently in use albeit for something different. The coal yard is still busy with a number of wagons in view and plenty of coal in stock. The erstwhile engine shed was situated just beyond the compound at the end of the former passenger platform near to where the previous image was captured. In 1971 the freight facilities were being run down as part of the BR strategy of the time was to rid itself of such traffic. At that time a Cl.08 DE 0-6-0 was employed for the daily chores. The line closed completely in December 1973.

Back on the ECML, we continue a few miles north to the next station, the last stop before Peterborough. Yaxley & Farcet is the station in question and on Saturday 4th April 1959 the last train to call, before closure on the following Monday, was the 1.35 p.m. King's Cross-Peterborough, which had brought us from Holme with 34A's Peppercorn A1 No.60139 SEA EAGLE doing the honours. This place, complete with its timber-built signal box, was opened in May 1890 as simply Yaxley; Farcet was added five years later. The station was actually situated approximately midway between the settlements of Yaxley (1792 souls) – one mile to the south-west – and Farcet (1243 souls) – one mile to the north-east. Obviously the larger village had its name used for the station but no doubt local opposition, and politics, had the smaller village name added later, after much protest. One alternative local name which may or may not have been a challenge to the eventual title was the name of the nearby water course which became the River Nene – Pig Water. The station was fully equipped with goods yard, shed and crane; the nearby brick works also had sidings just to the north, on the Down side.

Crescent Junction, Peterborough, Wednesday 23rd July 1958. *THE FLYING SCOTSMAN* is loaded to twelve bogies today, a comfortable load for Peppercorn A1 No.60149 AMADIS, one of the 'Top Shed' batch. This view shows the meeting of the lines from the east (GER), west (L&NWR, this company actually came in via a connection at Fletton Junction just south of this location), north (GNR and MR) and south (GNR). In the middle distance a WD 2-8-0 is slowly making its way towards the junction with a freight from the March direction via Peterborough East; to get onto this side of the main line it passed beneath the ECML prior to crossing over the river Nene. To the left of the WD is a somewhat crowded Nene carriage sidings. The skyline is punctured by numerous tall chimneys indicating the location of the various brickworks which dominated the landscape to the south of Peterborough.

We have no date for this view but it maybe the same day as the previous picture. Having cleared Crescent Junction, another Peppercorn A1 – they were so popular with BR around this time, I wonder why – No.60156 GREAT CENTRAL gets ready to negotiate the platform line through Peterborough (North) with the Down *TALISMAN*.

Peterborough (North) 12th June 1961. A3 No.60061 PRETTY POLLY (with wing deflectors fitted in November 1959, trying to sort out the double chimney smoke problem) has charge of the Down *WHITE ROSE* which it will be noted was without headboard. Note, beyond the North signal box, the bricked-up doorways to the former engine shed which had closed for business in GN days! Besides No.60061 having the wing deflectors fitted, No.60048, 60055 and 60112 also had the appendages.

Summer 1958 and the London-Edinburgh non-stop of its age, *THE ELIZABETHAN*, runs through Peterborough (North) with one of Haymarket's favourite A4s, No.60027 MERLIN in charge. The slack through the station here would have slowed the progress of the train quite a lot but the crew will soon have the whole thing wound up again by the time New England shed is passed. A young spotter clocks the number and notes it down – let's hope it was a cop.

What a sight! Immaculate A4 No.60021 WILD SWAN approaches Peterborough (North) with *THE ELIZABETHAN* on Friday 18th July 1958 with apparent consummate ease. This is where we take leave of this section of our imaginary journey along the East Coast Main Line from London to Edinburgh but our follow-up Part 2 will pick everything up here in Peterborough and whisk us further north. In the meantime let's just look to the immediate north for familiar landmarks: The arches of Westwood bridge span everything including the former Midland lines, the ECML and the various yards forming one long chain linking New England to the north and Peterborough itself. New England locomotive depot, situated on the east side of the ECML, is located by the massive 'Cenotaph' like coaling plant stuck out for all to see; the depot's water tower tries hard to compete. On the extreme right the new Peterborough goods depot is taking shape. More anon.